WALKING TOUCHING ON EARTH & THE SKY

WALKING ON EARTH

&

TOUCHING THE SKY

POETRY AND PROSE BY LAKOTA YOUTH
AT RED CLOUD INDIAN SCHOOL

Cataloging-in-Publication Data has been applied for and may be obtained from the Library of Congress.

ISBN: 978-1-4197-0179-5

Volume copyright © 2012 Timothy P. McLaughlin
Foreword copyright © 2012 Joseph M. Marshall III
Each poem copyright © 2012 its author, as identified at end of poem
Illustrations and captions copyright © 2012 S. D. Nelson

Book design by Maria T. Middleton

Printed and bound in China
10 9 8 7 6 5 4 3 2 1

Abrams Books for Young Readers are available at special discounts when purchased in quantity for premiums and promotions as well as fundraising or educational use. Special editions can also be created to specification. For details, contact specialsales@abramsbooks.com or the address below.

ABRAMS
THE ART OF BOOKS SINCE 1949
115 West 18th Street
New York, NY 10011
www.abramsbooks.com

JACKET ILLUSTRATION *Touching Hands*. Acrylic on Masonite, 14 x 20 in.

☼ Before going into battle, Lakota warriors tied eagle feathers in their horses' manes. Doing so gave their horses the power of the lofty bird. In like manner, they painted pictographs of lightning, which instilled the power of thunder; hailstones—fury; dragonflies—swiftness; and the sacred circle—immortality. Lastly, they painted their handprints upon their horses. This was more than a personal signature; it made the horse and rider one. —S. D. Nelson

To the students of Red Cloud Indian School:
Continue to make your voices heard, powerfully and perfectly.
With this book, I share what you entrusted to me.
May *Tunkasila,* our Grandfather, bless the offering.
Mitakuye Oyasin.

Thunder Dance. Acrylic on 140 lb. cotton paper, 21 x 29 in. The earth is pounding like a drum. Night's sky splits into day. In the land of visions, I dance the sacred way.

✿ For my Lakota people, the spirit world is as real as the physical world. We humans can touch both. It is common for us to go on a quest for a personal vision. By participating in traditional ceremonies, such as the *Hanblechia*, or Vision Quest, it is possible to glimpse and even enter the spirit world. —S. D. Nelson

CONTENTS

Sister Girl. Acrylic on Masonite, 24 x 30 in. Your face is smiling, cousin. I see the gift you bring.

☀ Horses were introduced to the Plains Indians by the Spaniards in the 1500s. Until that time, the Lakota roamed on foot, often using dogs to help carry their belongings. Horses were much bigger than the dogs and much faster. We Lakota called them *Shoon-ka Wakan*—Sacred Dog. They lifted us from the ground and carried us across the Great Plains. —S. D. Nelson

FOREWORD

EVERYONE HAS A VOICE THAT REVEALS A VERY INDIVIDUAL AND personal perspective on the issues and circumstances that affect him or her. Such is the case with the young people who have given us their voices in this book.

The words, the expressions, and the phrases you will read here are warm, hopeful, angry, sad, confused, insightful, and wise—but most of all honest. Too many times we grown-ups overlook the feelings and opinions of you, our children and grandchildren. When we do that, we are denying ourselves perspectives that complete the picture we have of the world around us. We all experience life at any age, as the young authors in this book so quietly, eloquently, and passionately show us.

Not only are the feelings and thoughts expressed intensely personal but they are also unique in that they reveal and represent the experiences of being Lakota in today's world. Any reservation is a homeland with a good side, a bad side, and a dimension somewhere in between. Reservations are probably the last strongholds of Native culture. One of the reasons is that today's grandparents and elders, like me, were born in the 1930s, 1940s, or 1950s and are the second or third generation to bear the brunt of assimilation. In spite of that, we have managed to preserve language, traditions, and customs to pass on to our children and grandchildren. Though a map identifies the parameters of the Pine Ridge Indian Reservation or the Rosebud, Cheyenne River, or Standing Rock Reservations, the rest of the world comes in whether we want it to or not. While reservations may be geographically isolated, they are very much part of the global community, owing to instant electronic communications. Consequently, there is a continuous assault on Native culture and identity. Yet, as the young people in this book demonstrate, the Lakota culture lives on within the reservation's boundaries. We grandparents are certainly proud, and so, too, are the generations before us who struggled to keep our identity.

No story is complete until all sides of it are heard. In the cacophony of voices from the world around us, these few young people from Red Cloud Indian School may be no more than a microscopic blip, but that does not diminish their message. They speak with an unblinking, honest humanity that serves as an example for anyone who wishes to stand up and be heard.

Though they may speak with youthful innocence, they also speak, because of that innocence, from the unvarnished reality of their place in the world. They are learning that a reservation is not only a homeland, it is also a proving ground.

For that reason, at the very least, we should listen to them.

So, in closing, I say to them, *Wasteyelo*. It is good.

Joseph M. Marshall III
Sicangu Lakota

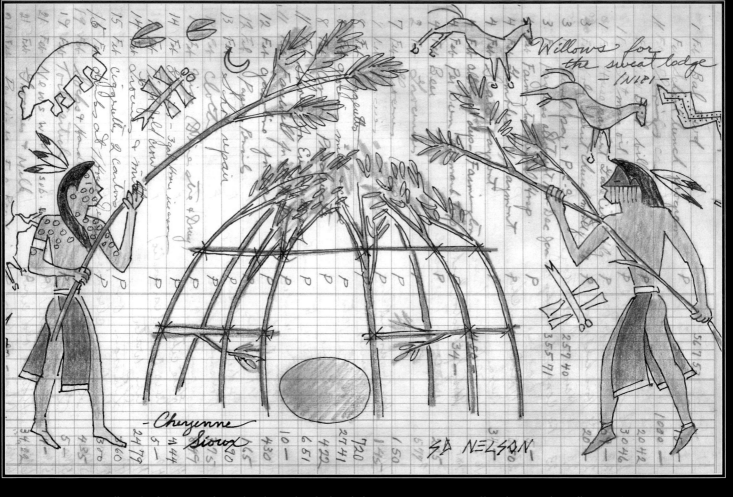

Willows for the Sweat Lodge. Colored pencil and ink on ledger paper, 14 x 8 in. We offer tobacco to the Willow People . . . and we say, "Thank you for helping us. You will become the ribs for our *inipi*."

☼ A sweat lodge, or *inipi*, is constructed from bent willow saplings and covered with robes or tarps. Stones are heated in a fire nearby until they glow from within. The stones are placed in a pit in the center of the lodge. People enter the structure on hands and knees, and then sit in a circle facing the holy Stone People.

In the late nineteenth century, Indians were given used (discarded) ledger books. With bold shapes and vivid colors, they drew on the lined pages, the images floating above the numbers and words. Sadly, the intentions of the bookkeeper and the Indian artist oppose each other; like oil and water, the two cultures never seem to connect. —S. D. Nelson

INTRODUCTION

THE LAKOTA PEOPLE, LIKE MANY NATIVE TRIBES, HAVE AN INTRICATE and fascinating history. Lakota creation stories speak of the people's emergence from Wind Cave in the Black Hills of South Dakota. Most scholars agree that the Lakota have lived for centuries in the northern Plains and Great Lakes areas of North America. Original Lakota life, before the time of Indian reservations, was organized by a circle of traditions that governed all aspects of human existence: shelter, food, clothing, family, milestones (birth, initiation, marriage, death), spiritual practices, and so on. The Lakota people's lifestyle was sustainable and in basic harmony with the land and other forms of life.

In the 1800s, European explorers arrived in the western United States. At the end of the century, the federal government established reservations, which sequestered tribal groups in specific territories. After a long series of military conflicts in defense of their original homelands, Chief Red Cloud and other Lakota leaders finally submitted to government-allotted territories in order to prevent the extermination of their people. Red Cloud was appointed leader at the Pine Ridge Reservation in South Dakota. He realized that traditional Native life was ending and that Lakota children would need to learn the ways of European Americans alongside their education in Lakota culture. So he petitioned the government to invite the Jesuits, whom he favored, to create a school on the Pine Ridge Reservation.

In 1888, the Holy Rosary Mission was founded on the site chosen by Chief Red Cloud. The history of the mission, like that of most Indian boarding schools, is checkered, with both dark and light pages. Much of the mission's intent in the early years was to assimilate Lakota children into mainstream society through conversion to Christianity and the learning of the English language. Today, the school is named

Red Cloud Indian School, and it has a different, redirected purpose: to facilitate an education of the mind and spirit that promotes both Lakota and Catholic values, a purpose likely much more in alignment with Red Cloud's vision for his children. Lakota culture and language are vital elements of the total curriculum, and the school is integrated into the pulse of the surrounding community.

Life on the Pine Ridge Indian Reservation is difficult and complex. Shannon County is the second poorest county in the United States, and conditions are very harsh. The people struggle with unemployment, poor housing, disease, alcohol and drug abuse, violence, depression, and more. Yet Lakota people are amazingly resilient and spiritually powerful. Among the Lakota, there is a tremendous love for the land, a system of profound cultural ways, a sense of community that often supersedes the struggles, and a capacity for humor as medicine for continuation and a source of joy.

Originally, the Lakota language was only spoken, not written. Lakota people recorded information and occurrences through pictographs, often drawn on buffalo hides, and they shared stories through the oral tradition, with elders serving as the storytellers for younger generations. Today, many Lakota youth are not entirely fluent in their Native language, and English has become the everyday language on much of the reservation. But the young people are still raised among a rich legacy of stories, some traditional and some more contemporary. Accordingly, Lakota youth are often adept listeners and have an intuitive sense of what makes a good story.

Their own stories spring from their multilayered identities. They are both young Lakota people, rooted in Native perspectives and ways, and regular kids navigating the present-day world. They might participate in traditional ceremonies, and they also surf the Internet. They may do beadwork or sing in Lakota, and, like all students in school today, they write. And their writing includes all components of their identities to create a unique and poignant artistic tapestry.

This book is a collection of writings by Lakota youth at Red Cloud Indian School. The selections come from a three-year period during which I taught reading and writing classes to students in the fifth through eighth grades. This volume aspires to honor these Lakota youth and their important words. I do not presume, nor is it necessary, that readers have an extensive knowledge of Lakota culture and philosophies. In many cases, the poems and writings may be read and interpreted as if written by young people of any background. However, each may also be read and understood from a Lakota or indigenous perspective. Therefore, I introduce each section of the book with some essential facts about the experiences and teachings these Lakota youth are drawing on.

The Creator blessed these young people with outstanding natural creativity brought forth amidst sometimes very difficult lives. Compiling this anthology has been, foremost, a gift to the Red Cloud students in recognition of my responsibility as the first caretaker of the expressions created in our classroom. Just as important, I hope these sacred words will find even greater life in the minds, hearts, and spirits of all those who receive them. ☀

A Note to the Reader

If more than one poem in a section has the same title, the title is only given once. The symbol ☀ represents the title of the following poem. The illustration captions are provided by the artist, S. D. Nelson. The title of the paintings, the specifications, and a reflection are given as one piece of text. Descriptive text follows, providing commentary on the art, or on the Lakota people.

Fire Chant II. Acrylic on Masonite, 36 x 48 in. Come, coyote brothers. Together we will sing up the stars. Yes, we will sing up the moon.

☼ Humans have known and used fire for ages. I believe our psyche is imprinted with the memory of gazing into the mesmerizing glow of fires from long ago. Like our ancestors, we still gather in the firelight to sing old songs. —S. D. Nelson

Four Elements

Wind blows. Fire burns. Water falls. Earth crumbles. The wind is the music that makes leaves dance. The fire is the transportation for things to go back to God. Water is the singing diamonds that take care of everything. Earth is the anchor for things.

—CARMEN FOURD

The Elements of Life

The wind is the motion of the spirits dancing in the spirit world, the sound of the buffalo running on the golden-yellow prairie. The fire is the symbol of the elders telling stories around the laughing campfire. The water is the symbol of eagles swooping down on the cool water on a hot summer day. The Earth is the symbol of the people of all colors—black, brown, white—all the animals, and all the green plants.

—KYLE WHITE

The Ocean

The ocean is the flow of the world
as we are the flow of nature
and its elements.

—DUNCAN DEON

Ocean and Sky

The sky is a copy of the ocean. Only it is upside down. The clouds are the waves that roll and toss about. The deep blue is the water, and all the birds are the fish in the ocean. The sky and the ocean are not different, really. They are quite the same, just in different places. Many people ponder about them both, looking for clues and answers.

—MEGAN WHITE FACE

The Sun

The sun is yellow and bright.
The sun goes in circles just for the night.
The sun is the biggest, most yellow star in the universe.
The sun stays in one place while we have to spin, spin, and spin.

—JESSIE STAR COMES OUT

Star

Star high in the sky, burning bright
The sun is coming up
At dawn, are you scared to burn
Right out of the night?

—JOYCE BUCKMAN

Dawn

The dawn is very beautiful with pink, dark blue, and yellow all spreading like watercolors. It is the beginning of a new day, a new life, a chance to start over again. Dawn is also something indescribable, a promise that there will be continuous life, as long as that star rises in the sky.

—CARMEN FOURD

Sunrise Morning

Sunrise morning. I like the purple orange sunrise. The way the dew drops off the leaves on the branches and onto your lawn and porch. The way the morning mist flows in the air. The purple clouds, the frost on the windows, half of the orange sun, the nice cool breeze.

—EUGENE GIAGO

Vowels and Colors

A, blue, is the color of the sky when clouds make weird shapes of animals and other things you can imagine.

E, red, is the symbol of dawn when the beautiful colors sprinkle over the hills with the scent of pine.

I, white, is the sign of snow, which falls through the air in the shape of a star with a mirror reflection.

U, green, is the shade grass where blossoms bloom and rabbits come to eat.

O, black, is the symbol of darkness when the cruel swims through mists of fog, the sign of death, when the good quivers amongst them.

—AMERY BRAVE HEART

Center of the World

I was looking into the sky at a mountain, thinking only time could destroy it. I climbed to the top. From there, I could see the ocean with waves gently washing over the shore. I could see the setting sun. In time, it would be dark. For now, it is light. I stand up there smelling the sweet brisk mountain air. When I stand here, I know I am in the center of the world.

—DAVID WOLFE

A Seed Is New Life

A single seed grows and becomes a tree for children to play on and climb.
A seed plants the grass that the deer and rabbits run on. A little seed plants
a forest. A single seed grew the whole world. A single seed grows and raises
each human or animal.

—KATHY McLAUGHLIN

Rose

soft and delicate
blooming with beauty
floating in stars

—JENNA TAPIO

What the Roses Are Saying

What the roses are saying cannot be heard through voice
but through beauty as you watch the rain slip
from their petals and hang from their edges.

—DENA COLHOFF

What the Clouds Are Saying

The clouds are saying I'm tired of looking down on this sick, sad world
with people killing, having babies, and violence.
I wish I could see a better tomorrow.
The clouds are sad, it's gonna rain.
The world is all pain like a stain that can't wash out.
I wish there was a better tomorrow, all I feel is sorrow.
I'm not happy with all this gossip and violence.
I'm gonna close my eyes, so I can drift away.

—KRISTIE TAPIO

Nature

I walk out into the open, never dreaming of what I'd see. I sat on a tree
and saw Mother Nature crying to me. When I looked around, I knew the
pain She felt. All the trees lifeless on the ground. She cries and asks me,
"How?" She continued, "It's gone. I had to say good-bye to my grass, trees,
and little animals, too. This was once beautiful and I was happy, but now
I feel like you."

—LARISSA ROSS

It's Peaceful in the Country

In the country, it's peaceful. The birds chirp a lot and make music. The wind blows like a smooth wave of the ocean. The horses and cattle run wild and free. When the wind blows, the weeds sway. When the sun shines, everything glows.

—BLUE DAWN LITTLE

Haiku

Nature is pretty
And beautiful comes out fast
It blooms without fear

—DUSTIN STAR COMES OUT

Spring

Spring is when you catch some good bass. Spring is when it starts to rain. Spring is when all the berries start to sweet. Spring is when it gets so hot that roads start to dry up.

—OJ TWO BULLS

Summer

Everything blooms. Dazzling colors explode across a green meadow. Little baby animals roam with their parents. Lots of memories come back to haunt and linger of summers past. Music blared across a town, trash cans exploding, fireworks going off. Then a little quieter, but not much. Still full of fun and happiness. Then it slips into fall. That's where the story ends.

—CARMEN FOURD

Metaphor

When you laugh, it's an echo of your past.
The moon is a round diamond.
The stars are pieces of memory.
The ocean is a blanket of dreams that lasts forever.
A rainbow is a bridge to your future.

—CLEMENTINE BOURDEAUX

Night

Night is dark but pleasant. It has a rhythm in the flow of the wind. The sky is like a chandelier of lights, high, high up beyond the clouds, which float like boats in water.

—DENA COLHOFF

Snowy Night

A snowy night is when my family is asleep and the coyotes are howling. I see the world through my window and it looks like a polar bear's back. The stars are bright and dogs are running around.

—DALLAS NELSON

Sunset and Stars

Sunset is like God reaching out and healing all that is sick.
Stars are the beaming madness brought out to all the messed-up world.
Sunset is beautiful colors settling on the horizon
waiting for the watchers to come out.
Stars are the watchers that look upon us and see nothing will happen to you.
Sunset and stars are like I wish I could live and look at it as a landscape.

—TYLER SEABOY

Nature

The sky is my mom watching over me.

The water is my memories to be.

Nature is my home and family.

—DERRICK McCAULEY

End of the Trail (after *End of the Trail* by James Earle Fraser). Acrylic on 140 lb. cotton paper, 21 x 29 in. Alcohol is a liar. For some, it is their God. For me, it is poison. I tell you the truth—I cannot drink it. I will not hold it up. I will not worship it.

Laughter

What is laughter? Is it the moment between reality and insanity? Or is it the true way to express yourself from all the torture you endured as a child when you look at your past and all you see are razor blades?

—RYAN ROSS

Loneliness

A time of sadness
A time away from your family
A time for being hurt
Being alone in a dark valley
Feeling lost in another world, but still in the same
You're alone in a dark, dark place

—ALISHA PATTON

Fear

cold and lost
quiet and dark
click, click and snap
night moon
are fear

—TIA CATCHES

Misery

Misery is when you go to eat somewhere, and two old white people are watching you. Misery is when you go to buy food, and they charge you extra. Misery is when you walk down the street, and there's an Indian and a white person fighting, and you know there won't be peace between the two. Misery is when you watch TV and see all the cowboys killing all the Indians. Misery is when people think Indians scalp everyone. Misery is going to a place, and everyone watches every move you make.

—JJ WILSON

✷

Indian misery is when somebody takes your land.
Indian misery is when somebody kills your friends.
Indian misery is when your people turn against you.
Indian misery is being slaves to people.
Indian misery is being locked up in jail.
Indian misery is people killing your food for money.
Indian misery is fighting. Indian misery is no peace.
Indian misery is when you get killed. Indian misery is if you lose the fight.

—ANDREW HERMAN

Misery is when you always seem to be getting dressed in black to go
to a funeral.
Misery is when you get there and realize that the person who is dead
is another close friend.
Misery is when you look around and all your friends are crying.
Misery is when you hear them say they'll try to stop
and stay away from this stuff.
Misery is when the next day you see them stocking up in White Clay
for a party soon to come.
Misery is when you hear the sirens, and you have to sit and wonder
whose funeral you'll be attending for the next few days.
Misery is when you realize they'll never stop,
and you'll always be choosing black clothing for the next day.

—KAYLA MATTHEWS

Cry

Cry makes me think of wakes and funerals. It's like you're trapped inside a small room and you can't breathe. So you cry. When you are helpless, you cry.

It's like you're sitting at a wake, and you're crying, and you can't do anything. Like a knife keeps stabbing your heart, over and over. You look around and everyone is crying. Your head is turning, and you feel like going up to the coffin and waking the person up, but it feels like your legs are tied down to the chair.

—JEANNIE TRUEBLOOD

Despair

Most of my life is despair.
It's to a point where I don't care.
I could just sit alone and watch cars go by.
I've been this way since the day my grandfather died.

I'd like to be like my dad, who is unafraid.
He is sharper than a razor blade.
Give me a paper and a pen
so I can write about my life of sin.

I feel like beating down someone with a chair
just to get rid of this despair.

—WALKER THOMPSON

Racism

Racism is a strong bullet through a person's heart.
Racism is like a bank with lots of unkind words.
Racism is like a gun in a child's hands
loaded with all the words a devil would say.

—JULIAN BEAR RUNNER

Still I Cry

They always treat me like the dirt. Like I'm some kind of beast.

They beat on me and don't treat me right.

So still I cry.

I say I'm the wind and I'm the dust. I watch the eagles fly.

They say I'm just a savage.

So still I cry.

They put me in a jail cell and laugh at my bare feet.

I didn't do anything wrong. They all just hate me.

Still I cry.

I cry at their light skin, their wrinkled faces, and evil eyes.

Still I cry.

I risk my life for one of them. I wish this racism will end.

They shoot me down and hang me up.

Still I cry.

I cry

I cry

I cry

I cry

As I am left here bound to die.

—KATHY McLAUGHLIN

Haiku

Tears fall from my face
As I walk the lonely grass
To a place unknown

—KRISTIE TAPIO

Moon of the Falling Leaves. Acrylic on 140 lb. cotton paper, 29 x 21 in. Beneath the cottonwoods, beneath the moon, I breathe the sweetness of falling leaves.

Being Indian

Being Indian means a lot to many Natives. Some people are so proud that they say "NP" or "Native Pride." A lot of people write this on their school papers or other things. Being Indian gives you the meaning of respect, generosity, courage, and wisdom. These things mean a lot when you are Indian. Many elders speak to young children about these four values, which still live in the Indian beliefs and are part of our culture. Indian clothing, tools, and marriages are still treasured today.

As an Indian, it takes lots of courage to stand up for yourself and others who are part of Indian culture. Like when prejudiced people say Indians are dirty and stink. A lot of people are like that in this world. That's why you have to stand up for yourself and others.

—ASHLEY JONES

☀

To me, being Indian means a lot because our ancestors were brave, courageous, and educated. Being an Indian means you have to stand up to people and demand respect because a lot of people stereotype Indians. Being Indian is an honor because long ago we were the only people who used the land in the right way.

Being Indian means you have to respect everyone because that's the way Indians are. Being Indian, you have to decide which way you want to live. To make it in the world, you have to be educated in the white person's way. Instead, you're an Indian and you want to live that way, but you can't.

—BLUE DAWN LITTLE

✵

Being Indian means respecting your elders and praying for your ancestors.
Being Indian means listening to your parents and being good to your
uncles and aunties. And most of all, being Indian means respecting
yourself, others, and Mother Earth.

—CANDIDA BAGOLA

✵

We Indians respect our land and buffalo. We know how to live and respect
others. The life we live now is different from the way it was long ago. We
have relatives who lived here and their spirits are flying all around us.

—SANDY RED FEATHER

✵

This is what an Indian means to me. An Indian is brave and he or she doesn't
care how you look. He or she gives instead of taking. They stand up to anything,
are ready for anything, and don't take anything for granted. They listen to other
people's needs and take care of what is sacred as well as everything else. They
pray for what they kill and use everything on the animals.

—DUSTY BLACK ELK

Circle

A circle is connecting at all times. A circle has no ends. A circle is round.
The world is a circle. Our life travels with a circle. A circle is strong. Strong
enough to hold together a tribe.

—RAYMOND GHOST BEAR

Every Little Dance

Every little dance is like the wind.
They are the gods running in the sky.
Every little dance is the drum beating.
The Indian dancers on the pow-wow grounds.
Every little dance creates a new world.
Every little dance is a new life.
Another baby comes into a person's life.

—ALISHA PATTON

Tradition

Tradition is a thing or a thought that lasts forever and ever.
Tradition is very special, and it will end never.
Tradition is my homeland, a very sacred place.
Tradition is my people, full of love and grace.
Tradition is what we believe in.
Tradition is the color of my hair, my eyes, my skin.
Tradition is the eagle feather.
Tradition is my loyal tribe. We will stick together.
Tradition is my family. Tradition is all of us.
Tradition is in me.

—KATHY McLAUGHLIN

✳

Tradition means passing something down, like a story. Something
that means something special to you. Your love to a child. As the child
remembers the love you gave to him, he passes it to his child. And so on.

—JENNA WARD

Courage

Courage is what our ancestors needed to live. It's how we survived. When
our people needed food in the freezing winter, some sacrificed their lives so
others could live. When someone was dying, it took courage to turn around
and help their family off the ground.

When we needed each other, we came and never left one to die. We
helped each other. Even though people tried to get us down, we never gave
up. We kept fighting. Lakota people are strong. It takes courage to keep
going.

—LARISSA ROSS

THE BATTLE

Through the hills and in the night,
I go straight to my final fight.
With my axe and bow in hand,
I ride across the forest land.

On my horse and in the moon,
I will see my battle soon.
As I look into the sky,
I sound my mighty battle cry.

Now the mighty battle starts,
I grow with courage in my heart.
As we attack the white man's station,
I know I am Sioux Nation.

—DAVID WOLFE

Ugly Life on Dirty Rez

Life on
Life on the reservation
Life on the reservation is dirty
Life on the reservation is dirty, filthy
Life on the reservation is dirty, filthy dogs.

—DENA COLHOFF

Animal Power

A butterfly is like a stained-glass window flying through the air. Sprinkling powers over children to make them laugh—happy and full of joy. A butterfly is a quiet yet graceful flying animal. The beautiful bright colors on its wings light up the morning sky. It is so delicate, it feels like powder. Its wonderful body just soars through the air. The wonderful body no child could resist. The antennae are like two little slivers stuck in its head. They make you dance and sing. They come in many shapes and sizes.

—ANNA DIAZ

Buffalo

Buffalo are powerful and graceful at the same time. A buffalo is like a fierce but beautiful wind. It protects its calf like a bumblebee protects its hive. It's swift as a butterfly but can sting like a bee. More like a thousand bees. I like it because it's important to my people, and it is also beautiful to watch.

—GABE MEANS

41

The Buffalo

I praise the buffalo, so strong. I kill him for food, good meat. I hunt him for his coat—so warm, so soft. He is my friend.

—KIRI HAMMOCK

White Buffalo

The white buffalos are saying, "I am the Great White Buffalo. I will go and roam the land, then I will go to sleep. Save your life and don't die."

—ASHLEY JONES

What the Birds Are Saying

They gave me advice. They said, "When you go and become the undead, you fly to heaven like us."

—LAIKEN LESSERT

Eagles

The eagles say to me, "The Great Spirit has come and told us what to do. We were sent by the Great Spirit to tell you stories and to protect you."

—SAMMIE TAPIO

Seven Ways of Looking at Eagles

One way is how he soars high above the clouds.

The second way is when the eagle sits on a tree branch

looking over the countryside.

The third way is when he grabs his prey on the prairie.

The fourth way is when his protective eyes are keeping you safe at all times.

The fifth way is when the eagle lets us borrow his feathers.

The sixth way is when he talks to the rest of the sacred animals

so they can also keep you protected.

The seventh way is how the eagle sits waiting for your own flight to the sky.

TONIA SCABBY FACE

Starbird. Acrylic on Masonite, 22 x 16 in. Our planet turns amidst the stars; the same stars seen by the old ones—the ancient people of our blood.

✺ As a boy, I looked up at the stars with a sense of wonder. Mom told me that the Milky Way was the White Road. She said that the lingering spirits of those who lived before us danced upon that road. —S. D. Nelson

Quiet

Quiet is the ringing in the ear.
Quiet is the pitch of the night.
Quiet is the feeling of relaxed.
Quiet is the soft touch of friends.
Quiet is the tenderness of babies sleeping.

—TIA CATCHES

Silence

Silence is the loudest noise I ever heard. The wind blowing gently across the prairie grass. The horses galloping around the field, the birds flying quietly to the trees. Silence is the loudest noise I ever heard.

—JULIA MARTIN

＊

Silence is the brushing leaves of a cottonwood on a cool spring day with the breeze through the grass. It is the nice damp dew washing pain from my soul. It is the soothing water running between my toes.

—TIA CATCHES

＊

Silence is when you're walking all by yourself thinking, listening to the wind blowing in your ears. Listening to the birds hum all day, hearing the water splash. Knowing that no one is around you, just nature and yourself.

EUGENE GIAGO

＊

Silence is the darkness of night when the moon shines bright and the pine trees make the only sound, the sound of a hundred cars on the freeway. Then, when the wind stops, there are no more cars, just silence.

—ISAAC RED OWL

✹

Silence comes when night covers the sky like a blanket, meaning it's time for everything to calm. Half the world is asleep, and everything is in silence. Silence comes when a close friend dies, and all you want is silence to be at your side and leave the other side to weep with tears.

— JEN GIAGO

✹

Like the time I walked up to my friend and all she did was cry. I felt really bad, but I didn't say a word. I hugged her and let her know that I cared. In some way, I knew she wasn't afraid. We didn't say anything, but silence fixed what I couldn't say.

— LARISSA ROSS

✹

Silence is when the last teardrop drips from your eyes. When the strong gentlemen help the coffin down into the hole as the family member who you will always love goes deeper and deeper into the ground. Others help to bury the loved one and burn sage or cedar to bless them. To show generosity and courage, family members drop a handful of misty dust over the coffin. To remember the person who was once alive, give a tear to the everlasting cries.

— ASHLEY JONES

＊

Silence is when I saw my mom for the last time. The air stopped, the people were silent, and my heart was still. Then I opened my eyes and saw that it was real. A world full of silence, I could hear no more. It was like I was on a beach and all I could hear were the waves coming onto the land. Then I saw her hand. She took me to a place of nonbelief. I saw the world of silence and peace.

—DERRICK McCAULEY

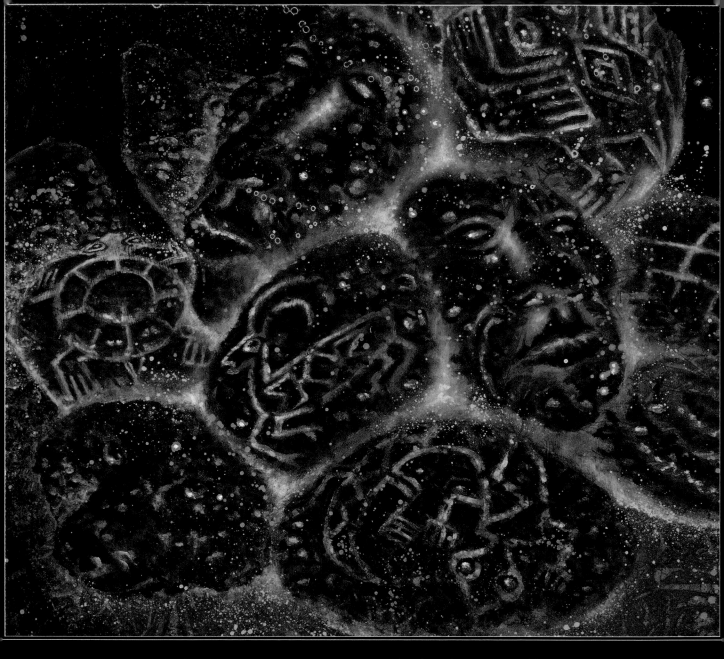

Stone People. Acrylic on Masonite, 24 x 30 in. Because some would not listen, because they could not see; in turn, a gift was given—the Stone People chose me.

☼ We are taught that upon entering the sweat lodge we are returning to the womb of mother earth. The Stone People are there in the black void. In the center of all things they glow with wisdom and offer a teaching. —S. D. Nelson

Vision of God

My vision of God is a spirit moving with us through every step we take along our path of life. He is in every living thing, in the trees, helping them move their leaves, in a rock, helping it live. He is in us, helping us paint all the colors of the world.

He lives in us as we cross the beating sunset. He is with us through the coming moon. He is there when we hear the rivers roar. The Great Spirit is there when love and hate is in the painting winds.

—ANNA DIAZ

✷

God is everything that can nourish us. He's in the sun, which gives us life and power. He's in the elk and buffalo, which give us food to survive. He's in the vegetables and fruit to keep us healthy. He's all around for someone to talk to. He's there when we need help with something. He's around us answering our prayers. God is my Dad and Mom.

—EUGENE GIAGO

✷

My vision of God is all around us. He looks like a tree with His arms stretched out protecting us from the sun. God is like the moon giving us light to see at night. The Earth is God's face showing all over the place.

—SANDY RED FEATHER

*

I see God, He is like the Earth. He's like the rivers, lakes, and sea. I know one thing for sure, He's in me, He's in everybody. He loves, cares, and gives. He gave us lives to live and live. He gave us the Earth to take care of, but we messed up. There's sin with you and me and everybody.

—DANI STEELE

*

My vision of God is a little boy standing on the curb, waiting for his mom, an old lady trying to find a bite to eat. A person on the streets trying to make it through the night. I see God in everything that I see every day, and I know God is in me.

—KYLE WHITE

*

My vision of God is a little kid playing in the dirt. He is inside of me. God is the dirt the kid plays in. He is everything around the kid. He is the toys the kid plays with. He is the blue sky above him. He is the school the kid goes to. God is love in the kid and everyone else in the world.

—MIKE KOCER

*

My vision of God is an Indian with his face painted like a warrior who went back in time and helped us be free and get our land back. He made it so white people won't kill all the Indians. He has a lot of muscles.

—TYLER LITTLE FINGER

✹

I vision God standing in the rain. He is in the rainbow waving, making pretty bright colors: pink, blue, orange, yellow. He is holding out his hand to the spirit eagles dancing around near him. The bears hollering. The bold eagles flying in a circle. The eye of a fish glowing.

—SAMMIE TAPIO

Being Alone

Being alone is like being with your inner spirit. You're in the dark, and the wind just shatters your sweat. Then, when the light comes on, you come out of your dream.

—BLUE DAWN LITTLE

What the Spirits Are Saying

They tell us when danger is near by using the wind, snow, and all weather. They tell us by letting us feel their presence or by a creature that we never saw before. Or by just letting us see them.

—MORRIS WARD

Faith

They say home is where the heart is,
so my home must not be here.
For my heart is in a place called Faith.
A small but lovely place
with trees to climb,
and fields to play in,
and friends to fight and forgive.
Friends that will always be there.
So if home is really where the heart is,
my home is far, far from here.

— KAYLA MATTHEWS

Three Haiku

The night of the death
Open your heart to the world
Only God knows why

— ALISHA PATTON

A thousand years old
And moves faster than I do
And whispers live long

— STEPHANIE SULLY

*

I am spiritual,
Meaning very strong inside,
Not hurt easily

—DERRICK McCAULEY

After Death

After death to me is on the plains with mountains around the village. There are tipis, people laughing and enjoying themselves. Whatever they want is there. I imagine God, *Tunkasila*, as an Indian walking around. Talking to people. Everything I loved that died is there. That's how I imagine the next world.

—EUGENE GIAGO

Death

People die in a quick history. When you hear, it's like a mystery. I see people's shoulders drooping like teardrops. Dying is like a blackout. When you arrive, it's like a whiteout. I pray day and night I won't go the next day. When you get in trouble, you have to pay. Sometimes when I awake, I think it's all a dream. The sun and the stars are like dreams. People saying why. I hear little people saying goodbye. The flowers are blooming. And the night is glooming. Babies are born. Humans are dying every day. People are torn in two.

—TYLER SEABOY

WORDS OF LIFE AND DEATH

The words of life are words of joy,
but the words of death are sad and lonely.
And often, death is soft and peaceful,
and life is often stale.

—TIA CATCHES

I've Got Your Back. Colored pencil and ink on ledger paper, 8 x 14 in. With a sober heart I am standing. With clear vision I see. I depend on you. You depend on me.

✿ All these traditions and old teachings are like tools. They serve no purpose until we pick them up and use them. —S. D. Nelson

All My Relatives

All of my relatives are like the wild prairies, different sizes that are old and new. We are like the stars, there are a great many of us. We are like the sea, we have many voices. We are like the skies, always changing from beautiful to ugly and mean. Some of us are like the trees, very old and wise. The rest of us are like the flowers, still young and learning.

—KATHY McLAUGHLIN

Family

In a family, there are a lot of things:
mothers, fathers, brothers, sisters, aunties, uncles, cousins, nephews, nieces,
in-laws, outlaws.
Problems, answers, confusion, laughter, horror, and more problems.
And when you don't know, you love them.

—DUNCAN DEON

Mother

Your mother is always there, even if you're miles apart. Your mother is your heart. Mom understands, no matter the situation. Your mother lets you go when you're in a bad mood. Your mother is there when you're feeling sad, depressed, and afraid. Your mother is like your guardian angel. She watches you. She's there.

—KRISTIE TAPIO

Relations Write

Me and my mom are like a tree, a tree that got cut down and made into paper with us glued down on it. My mom on the left and me on the right. That paper got ripped between left and right, knocked on the floor, and taken up and away to the trash. Then someone came to take out the trash, and when we got to the dump, the trash bag ripped. There I went into the wind, and it dropped me on the ground. More wind came and took me, and I never saw my mom again.

—DUSTY BLACK ELK

Still I'm Loved

When I do something bad, still I'm loved.
When I'm crabby and mad, still I'm loved.
When I stomp around, still I'm loved.
When I beat people up, still I'm loved.
When I do drugs and throw trash around, still I'm loved.
When I die and move away, still I'm loved.

—RAYLEEN BICKERSTAFF

LOVE

Boats sailing away forever and ever.
They never stop, always sailing.
Being lost, alone and happy,
Together forever and always in peace.

—TIA CATCHES

WHO AM I?

I am a rose in a patch of weeds.

I am a storybook mixed in with some dictionaries.

I am a chokecherry bush surrounded by oak trees.

I am a window that is broken.

I am a boy with lots of sisters.

I am an Indian surrounded by white people.

I am a football player at a basketball game.

I am a cat with a bunch of dogs.

I am an angel around a lot of devils.

I am a Walkman at a rock concert.

I am a block that tries to fit into a circle.

—DUSTY BLACK ELK

✸

I am the wings of a butterfly, colorful and happy. I am the big blue sky, always wondering why. I am the mud you step on after it rains. I'm nothing but a big stain. I am the basketball bouncing on the floor. I am the slamming door. I am nothing.

—KRISTIE TAPIO

To Be a Kid

To be a kid, it's like being strong and being tough. You have to stand up for what you believe in and what's right. People try to push you around, but you gotta tell them that you're your own self. People try to force you to do drugs. Sometimes you do it, sometimes you don't. I guess it all depends on the person you are and the person you want to be.

Being a kid is like being in your own world and making your own decision. What happens to you when you're a kid sticks with you in your future. Whatever you want to do is what you're gonna do. Your parents can try to help you, but they can't keep you locked up in a cage. When you're a kid, you gotta be like a kid or be the way you want.

—BLUE DAWN LITTLE

✺

To be a kid is like being your own boss. It is hard here and there. Grown-ups are too strict, nobody will get off your back. Sometimes, you feel the world is against you and you can't trust anybody. Sometimes, you're so bored, you feel like you're seventy or something. Sometimes, you just want your own space to get your head together. Sometimes, you wish you lived in a bigger city. Sometimes, you feel like everybody's out to get you.

—CURTIS RED OWL

✺

To be a kid is like having no responsibilities and not having to worry about anything. It's all about you and what you want, but to you, nothing really matters. Everything is all just fun and games, but as you get older you gradually lose the insight of being a kid, and everything starts to matter.

—EARL BREWER

To Be a Teen

Being a teen is hard these days. It is easier to get a hold of drugs and shots, and the cars go by like mosquitoes looking for blood. Not too much happens physically, but mentally is where most of the damage takes place. The hurt inside builds up so much that you can't think at all. Sometimes it gets so great that we search for help, but most of us never find it.

—TAMI MATTHEWS

I feel the world looking at me with evil jealous eyes. People are jealous of me because I don't run around and start fights and make enemies. I watch TV and see people across the world who don't have anything at all: no food, no clothes, no nothing. At night, when I think of them, I hear their dying cries. I live in a world filled with loneliness, hatred, and jealousy, but there's a whole new generation who could do something about that.

I have fun and don't worry sometimes. I like to live in excitement and do this and that. To be a teen is hard. I don't think I would get through all my days without a friend beside me. I want the world to see me as me, and I want the world to let me be.

— STEPHANIE SULLY

Dreams and Reality

A dream is something great you hope may happen someday. A vision you see in your imagination. Everything seems perfect. It's utopia. Everything is delicate and delightful. Reverie. Fantasies filled with love, freedom, justice, and peace.

Reality is the real life we're in now. Hatred, evil, war, injustice, slavery, starvation. Homeless, poor. Things happen in this world that aren't worth living for. Suicides are because of these things. Families split up and killings go on. I wish everyone could live in a dream.

— KATHY McLAUGHLIN

Dreams of the Babies

Young, sweet, innocent souls dreaming of how they came to be. Sleeping in their beds with the moon, stars, sun, and clouds hanging over their heads. Hate, jealousy, envy, racism, and sin revolving in the world, but they have no clue of it. They just know when to smile, cry, laugh, and play.

They know when others are asleep because everything gets quiet. They don't hear any old, odd voices. They dream of all the things heaven wants them to. When they awaken with a cry, the angels are there to comfort them and make them smile and laugh.

—STEPHANIE SULLY

I Have a Dream

I have a dream that one day everybody will get along. I have a dream that someday a lot of people will come from all around the world and get together and rebuild homes, schools, old buildings and turn them into something. I have a dream that one day the world will be a better place. I have a dream that one day Pine Ridge and Oglala will be good, healthy, strengthening, and protective communities.

—ANNA DIAZ

☀

I have a dream that one day Indians will be treated with real respect. Not just Indians, but all people. Whether they're black, white, brown, fat or thin, they would all be treated with respect.

—KIRI HAMMOCK

Freedom

Freedom is coming to school every day, knowing you'll get an education to go on. Going on to another grade until you graduate college. Freedom is when you're told you aren't going to get off the rez, but believing you're going to be the first Indian woman president, and maybe you'll make a difference.

—CHANDA THOMPSON

Still I Dream

There are people putting drugs in their bodies
and trash all over the ground.
But still I dream good dreams.
There are people dying.
But still I dream about the past and how happy we were.
People are starving and have no home.
But still I dream all of us are a family,
and we each have food and a home to live in.

—CHANELLE DOUVILLE

Thunder Drum. Acrylic on 140 lb. cotton paper, 21 x 29 in. All are welcome in this circle, where old songs become new.

☀ For some, thunder and lightning are frightening. In Lakota teaching, they are reassuring. They demonstrate the awesome sacred power in creation. We like it when storms come. —S. D. Nelson

The Writer

The writer can make any time, place, or person beautiful. A writer can control people's thoughts and emotions. The writer is a person who takes time to group words to make changes.

—LARISSA ROSS

✳

The poet is like the spirits. They both help people make right decisions. You can feel them inside your body. With the poet, his words are what you feel.

—CHANELLE DOUVILLE

Writing

I feel good writing. You write fast or slow, and you get an image of that. You could say that I have an imagination or a wide mind. It's kind of hard. I think it's easy.

—DUNCAN DEON

✳

Writing is like flowing water. As your ideas pour onto the paper, it is almost like the way water flows in a river. Going on and on in a constant stream of ideas being transformed into letters and words.

—JON DECKER

Art

Art
Art is
Art is pure
Art is pure and
Art is pure and good.

—SONNI RICHARDS

Why Do I Write?

When I write, it comes from my heart. When I write from my heart, I do not want to stop. I want to write until I pop. When I write from my heart, nothing but the truth comes out. I can make up stories with my mouth, but not on paper. When I write, it's like a dream.

—DUSTY BLACK ELK

✵

I write to get away from the world, to be on my own for just a little while. I write to get all my feelings into just one sentence. I write to remember that day forever. I write for the fun of writing.

—CHRISTINA CORDIER

✳

I write to get all the hate, bad, and not good stuff out of me. I just want something to do. I want to let all my good thoughts go on paper. I want to experiment with all the words. I wish to accomplish something by writing.

—TONY WEASEL BEAR

Freedom

Everyone has freedom, no one can take it away from you. People can chain you and make you work until you almost die. They can take everything away from you but not the most important freedom. That freedom is the will to live in other worlds and imagine other things, to live in fantasy and forget reality. That freedom is something no one can chain to walls or beat. That freedom is invincible and will live forever, never die.

—BRANDON HOOPER

Imagination

Imagination is when your thoughts bring you into a new world. Like when you see a butterfly flutter in the sky as your tears begin to dry. Imagination is when the real world is abandoned by your heart. Like when you imagine that your heart takes apart the colors of the rainbow. Imagination is when I'm bored, have nothing to do, and go in search of something to write about. Like when I sit and daydream about unicorns, beautiful waterfalls, and an eagle flying through the sky.

—ASHLEY JONES

✷

Imagination is the sea of colors that flows in your mind. Imagination is the pinkish orange of dawn and the bluish purple of sunset. Every day—sunset, sunrise, sunrise, sunset. Feeding your soul and watering your mind. The soundproof dimension in which you live at night. Where anything you want is yours and is. Imagination is the key of everything that was and is to be.

—CARMEN FOURD

✷

Imagination
Will always exist for me
Never dies for kids

—ISAAC RED OWL

White Buffalo II. Acrylic on Masonite, 30 x 24 in. White Buffalo—my vision does remain. My bitter heart made gentle—teardrops in the rain.

☀ The White Buffalo is rare among all his dark brothers and sisters. For Lakota people, the White Buffalo is sacred and the incarnation of goodness. —S. D. Nelson

ACKNOWLEDGMENTS

I THANK ALL THE YOUNG AUTHORS AND THEIR FAMILIES FOR THEIR support of this project and their courage to participate in it.

I extend my deepest gratitude to the community of Red Cloud Indian School for nurturing a safe and open educational environment where students can invent freely with language.

I hold special appreciation for two mentors who guided me in the effort to make this book in a way that respects and honors the Lakota people. *Pilamaya yelo,* Basil Brave Heart and Wilmer Mesteth.

And I am humbly grateful to you, Joseph Marshall, for offering your wisdom to me and to all of us.

Great thanks also to Howard Reeves for his intelligent suggestions and steadfast faith in this book.

Eternal love and thanksgiving to my family, always my source and foundation.

Above all, highest praise to *Tunkasila,* Grandfather. You blessed the students and me in this portion of the journey and continue to open the sacred red road before me. ☀

Storm Rider. Acrylic on 140 lb. cotton paper, 24 x 30 in. Courage will be given . . . if you seek it.

☀ Crazy Horse painted a lightning bolt down his face and chest. He dabbed spots of color on his body to represent hailstones. Our leader faced storms by becoming like a thunderstorm himself. —S. D. Nelson

AUTHOR'S NOTE

I HAD THE SUPREME HONOR OF LIVING AND TEACHING AMONG THE Lakota people through a volunteer program at Red Cloud Indian School. I taught reading and writing classes, coached basketball and soccer, and even drove a school bus. My experience powerfully shaped the direction of my life, as I have now taught in Native communities for thirteen years. My path is not entirely surprising, because my great-great-grandparents, Florence Isabel Leslie and Harry Jourdan Kilgour, moved westward from Virginia in the late 1800s to teach and work on an

Indian reservation. My great-grandmother, Louisa Jourdan Kilgour, was born in Fort Simcoe, Washington, on the Yakama Reservation, and grew up until age thirteen with Native people, probably leading a fairly indigenous lifestyle. As a boy, I knew none of this, but my great-grandmother's deep and fierce presence influenced me greatly. I believe that she bequeathed a spiritual inheritance to me: an affinity for and connection to Native peoples and ways.

When I first arrived in South Dakota (coming from Virginia, like my great-great-grandparents), I was excited to try my hand at teaching writing. I believe passionately in the value of creative expression through language, and I aspired to make the classroom a place where students could utilize writing to openly explore both their inner selves and their experiences of the world. I was twenty-two and a very recent college graduate, and I was equipped with more enthusiasm than savvy and didn't fully realize the scope of this ambition.

On the first day of my teaching career, it became immediately apparent that the students were much less interested in what we would do in class than in who I was, and, foremost, whether I could survive in this reservation school. It was equally clear that they would not do anything of true substance under my guidance until they knew and trusted me. Really, this was their world, and I was their guest. I had to demonstrate that my heart was good and my character strong before the students would share their stories around me.

After a long process of building mutual respect (a process I view as both a mystery and yet very genuine), our classroom became a place where the kids felt safe to explore, create, and share—an environment that consistently encouraged them to find their voices and express them joyfully. That environment was created principally from positive group experiences with writing. My job, as it revealed itself to me, was to develop prompts that spoke to the students, require and honor silent concentration during composition, model respect for everyone's expressions, honestly compliment their writing efforts, and enthusiastically facilitate sessions of sharing work aloud. As a new teacher, I was no master at any of this, but I did recognize, and then lovingly hold, the intense and holy energy that rose when the kids really dove in and shaped their stories.

As the students engaged with writing, their creative voices appeared and began to mature. At first, a few lines or images here and there would resonate as strong work. Soon enough, they were crafting short poems or statements that flowed well, demonstrating ability in diction and figurative language, and communicating something substantial. I realized these Lakota youth had important, real things to say and a natural ability to articulate them beautifully. It made sense that in the unpredictability of reservation life, where things seldom follow any rigid structure, the young people responded well to creative, open-ended assignments. I also believe that enduring the hard realities of reservation life built inner reservoirs of strength in the Red Cloud students. Through suffering, they gained an early authority to speak and be heard.

Once they had discovered this freedom to open themselves, they ran with it. Over time, I witnessed a transformation: from the motionless bodies and hard faces of the first day to students who would begin class with a smile and a laugh, get to work and produce something meaningful, and finally even read it aloud. I needed only to open the doors of self-expression, and then mainly get out of the way, as the students rushed through the threshold into the chambers of creativity where they did amazing things with, around, and through language. With this book, I honor these Lakota youth who both walk on Earth and touch the sky, and whose writing speaks from the spirit. ☀

INDEX OF TITLES

INDEX OF POETS